Thomas Paine and the Fight for Liberty

Leaders of the American Revolution

Leaders of the American Revolution

Thomas Paine and the Fight for Liberty

Samuel Willard Crompton

CHELSEA HOUSE
PUBLISHERS
A Haights Cross Communications ✦ Company ®
Philadelphia

CHELSEA HOUSE PUBLISHERS
VP, NEW PRODUCT DEVELOPMENT Sally Cheney
DIRECTOR OF PRODUCTION Kim Shinners
CREATIVE MANAGER Takeshi Takahashi
MANUFACTURING MANAGER Diann Grasse

Staff for Thomas Paine and the Fight for Liberty
EXECUTIVE EDITOR Lee Marcott
EDITORIAL ASSISTANT Carla Greenberg
PRODUCTION EDITOR Noelle Nardone
PHOTO EDITOR Sarah Bloom
COVER AND INTERIOR DESIGNER Keith Trego
LAYOUT 21st Century Publishing and Communications, Inc.

A Haights Cross Communications ✦ Company ®

www.chelseahouse.com

First Printing

9 8 7 6 5 4 3 2 1

Library of Congress Cataloging-in-Publication Data

Crompton, Samuel Willard.
   Thomas Paine and the fight for liberty/Samuel Willard compton.
      p. cm.—(Leaders of the American Revolution)
   Includes bibliographical references and index.
   ISBN 0-7910-8625-9 (hard cover)
   1. Paine, Thomas 1737–1809—Juvenile literature. 2. Political scientists—United
States—Biography—Juvenile literature. 3. Revolutionaries—United States—
Biography—Juvenile literature. 4. United States—History—Revolution,
1775–1783—Juvenile literature. I. Title. II. Series.
   JC178.V5C76 2006
   320.51'092—DC22

                                                      2005004816

Contents

The
Crisis

It was the third week of December 1776. The soldiers of the Continental Army were hungry and cold. Sometimes they did not have enough to eat. And these were the men who had to win America's freedom. If they did not do it, no one else could.

George Washington led his tired and ragged men on the south bank of the Delaware River. As they stared across the river, already caked with ice, the Americans could see smoke and perhaps even smell the fires of their enemies. These enemies were well fed and had warm houses in which to sleep.

In 1776, the war for America's independence was in its second year. The fighting that began at Lexington and Concord in Massachusetts had lasted a long time. Some of the men under General Washington had been in the war from the beginning. Others had signed up more recently. But everyone knew that no one would sign up right now. The cause was too desperate, and defeat seemed likely.

It was a time of deep and painful crisis. The Americans had lost New York City to the British in September. Then they had been defeated at White Plains and had lost Fort Washington and Fort Lee. Now they were on the south bank of the Delaware River, with little left to lose.

It was the darkest of times for George Washington, the commander-in-chief of the Continental forces. In a letter to a friend, he confessed his belief that unless something really good happened very soon, the fight for American liberty would be lost.

HOPE IN A TIME OF CRISIS

In this darkest of times, the third week of December, in the second year of the war, George Washington received a bit of encouragement. It came from the writing of Thomas Paine. This American journalist had just published a new pamphlet called "The Crisis."

As he read Paine's words, George Washington felt something he had not felt in a long time—hope. But hope must be acted upon to turn it into reality. And that was what Washington realized. He must act. His men must act. The time was now.

Knowing the importance of morale, General Washington ordered his captains to take a copy of Paine's pamphlet. *The Crisis* was read aloud to each brigade and each company in the Continental Army. A total of about 3,500 men heard the words of Thomas Paine read aloud in that bitterly cold third week of December.

Paine's pamphlet began with a sentiment with which the soldiers could identify: "THESE are the times that try men's souls." [1]

Thomas Paine's writing inspired many Americans during some of the most challenging days of the Revolutionary War.

All of the soldiers had felt that sense of deep despair Paine described. But to hear the words made it different. Somehow, the struggles of each and every man were made more real.

The pamphlet continued: "The summer soldier and the sunshine patriot will, in this crisis, shrink from the service of his country. . . ."[2]

The words must have embarrassed those of the men who longed to be a "summer soldier," who had already gone home, or a "sunshine patriot" who did not fight in the dark of winter. "But he that stands it now," Paine wrote, "deserves the love and thanks of man and woman."[3]

There was something different about those words. Man and woman. Only a man like Thomas Paine, raised in the Quaker faith, would have written "man and woman." Other authors would have left it at "man."

Paine's pamphlet continued: "Tyranny, like hell, is not easily conquered; yet we have this consolation with us, that the harder the conflict, the more glorious the triumph. What we obtain too cheap, we esteem too lightly."[4]

Every man in Washington's camp probably felt a chill at these words. These men were inspired. The power of words, produced on paper, and reproduced by voice, had shown their great strength.

There was more, much more, to *The Crisis*, but much of its power came from its very first words: "THESE are the times that try men's souls."

What would these men do with this new inspiration? Who was the man who had given it to them?

Test Your Knowledge

1 In December 1776, Washington led his men across which river before attacking enemy troops in New Jersey?

    a. The Susquehanna River.

    b. The Delaware River.

    c. The East River.

    d. The James River.

2 Where were the first battles of the Revolutionary War fought?

    a. In Massachusetts.

    b. In New York.

    c. In Virginia.

    d. In Pennsylvania.

3 What was the title of the pamphlet by Thomas Paine that Washington gave to his captains in December 1776?

    a. *War and Peace.*

    b. *The Struggle for Independence.*

    c. *The Crisis.*

    d. *Liberty and Freedom.*

8 Thomas Paine and the Fight for Liberty

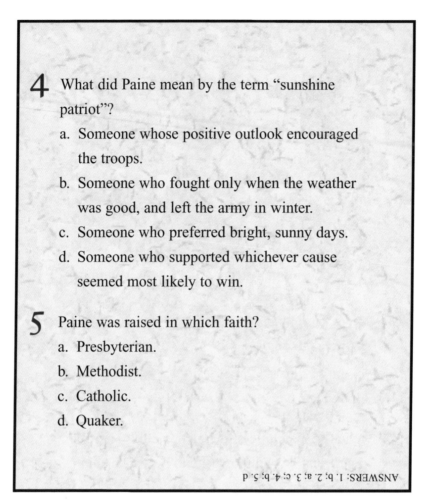

4 What did Paine mean by the term "sunshine patriot"?
   a. Someone whose positive outlook encouraged the troops.
   b. Someone who fought only when the weather was good, and left the army in winter.
   c. Someone who preferred bright, sunny days.
   d. Someone who supported whichever cause seemed most likely to win.

5 Paine was raised in which faith?
   a. Presbyterian.
   b. Methodist.
   c. Catholic.
   d. Quaker.

English
Youth

William Shakespeare, the great English poet, offered this prescription for achievement: "Do not fear greatness, for some are born great, some achieve greatness, and others have greatness thrust upon them."[5] Thomas Paine probably belongs in the second category. He was a person who achieved greatness through trial, turmoil, and effort. In this, he was like George Washington, the Continental Army's commander-in-chief. Both men had to go through many mistakes and trials before they reached their true greatness.

It is well known that George Washington was born in Virginia in 1732. We still celebrate his birthday today, on Presidents Day, which comes in the middle of February. We can chart his rise from young boy to military adventurer, to farmer, to American president. But Thomas Paine's life offers a portrait of a man who followed a very different path to fame and greatness.

Thomas Paine was not born in America. He was born in Thetford, England, on January 29, 1737. This made him about five years younger than George Washington. There was a great ocean between these two men, and their youthful experiences were quite different.

Thomas Paine was the only son of Quaker parents. Quakers was a term used to describe members of a religious sect whose beliefs included the idea of equality of the sexes and equality of people everywhere. The Quakers believed in things that Americans now hold dear, but very few people agreed with them in the 1700s.

In 1737, the year Thomas Paine was born, most English people believed in a social order that was based on vertical principles. This meant that some people were higher than others, some were lower than others, and some people were in the middle. This is different from the horizontal type of society Americans believe in today. The principle that all people have certain rights, rights that cannot be taken from them, was quite foreign in England in the early part of the eighteenth century.

We do not know that much about Thomas Paine's early years. He seems to have been close to his father and rather distant from his mother. But he did receive the Quaker teachings they believed in, and from an early age he believed in the basic equality of humans everywhere. This alone made him different from many others.

TAX COLLECTOR

Thomas Paine's father was a maker of stays, which means he helped to make clothes. This was a job people did in their homes. They did not have to go far away to work, but they did have to produce, and to produce a lot in order to make enough money to live.

Thomas Paine learned his father's trade. As he grew up, Thomas Paine came to know the hard labor it took to make a living. Perhaps he wanted an easier life for himself. As a teenager, he applied to become an excise man.

Excise means "use" and excise taxes are "use taxes." This means that you are taxed on the use you get out of something. Then, as now, excise taxes were

England in Thomas Paine's Youth

She was the greatest naval and commercial power the world had ever seen. No other empire had ruled the waves and controlled commerce the way that England did in the mid-eighteenth century.

Only 100 years earlier, England had been strong, but not mighty. Her European neighbors—France, Spain, and Holland—had kept her in check. But in the 1750s, the British fought the long French and Indian War (they called it the Seven Years' War) and emerged as the great victors. They obtained Canada and other French-controlled territories. They came out with the best and strongest navy. British ships carried British goods around the world.

But, as we've seen, things were not so good for Thomas Paine and for many other Englishmen. It was as unpopular. You had to be a rather daring man to go out and collect these taxes. Paine's life as an excise man would not necessarily be easier than that of his father, but it would involve more adventure and danger. People often refused to pay their excise taxes, and Paine would have to go to extraordinary lengths to collect the owed payment.

if the great success of England abroad took attention away from the needs of the people at home. The 1760s were a decade of poor harvests and high prices for food. Men and women like Thomas Paine were unable to get enough to eat, much less to share in the glories of the British Empire.

Ironically, the period of England's greatest success coincided with a time of trouble for its ordinary citizens. This was made clear by the number of people who left the country to live elsewhere. Thomas Paine went to America in 1774. Many other Englishmen followed him once the American Revolution was over. In the 1790s, many Englishmen went, or were forced to go, to Australia. Canada, America, Australia, and other lands all benefited from the discontent in England.

Thomas Paine did not do well in his new job. He found that there were many expenses involved in the work, and that the British government did not repay all of the money he spent. Even so, he did not quit his job, but instead was fired from it. And once this happened, he tried to get his job back, several times.

When he was fired, Thomas Paine went home to Thetford. He returned to work with his father in the business of making stays. It was no doubt a depressing time for the young man, who had hoped to succeed in his chosen career and see a bit more of the world, and instead found himself back home, working for his father.

During this time, Paine experienced the fate of many eighteenth-century Englishmen, who found it impossible to rise above a certain point, or to break free from the life and type of work their parents had known. Indeed, most Englishmen were suspicious of those who tried to rise above the circumstances into which they had been born.

During his years as an excise man and as a clothing maker, Thomas Paine read as much as he could. The business of printing and the making of books had boomed and there were more books than ever before.

Paine worked first as a tax collector and then made stays before traveling to London to become a journalist.

Thomas Paine loved words. He loved to test them on the tip of his tongue, to see how they sounded. He experimented all the time.

CONFLICT IN THE COLONIES

During these years, the decade of the 1760s, America and England were at odds with each other. England had sent out colonists a long time ago. Those colonists had created the 13 American colonies, which stretched from

New Hampshire in the north to Georgia in the south. But as the years went by, a new generation was born— a generation of young men and women who did not remember life in England, who felt close ties to their individual colonies, rather than faraway England. Even the type of language they spoke was a little different from that spoken in the streets of London.

So, by the 1760s, the colonists were as aware of what separated them from England as of what tied them to the British Empire. They still believed in certain basic English principles, in fundamental English law, in trials by jury. But what soon divided them was a matter Thomas Paine knew something about: taxes.

The English had always had taxes. They had people who represented them, in the House of Commons. These people decided which items would be taxed and by how much.

The colonists had their own taxes, designed to support their colonies, but had never paid taxes to England. All that changed in the 1760s, when England began placing taxes on tea, lead, paper, paint, glass, and stamps.

The British Parliament believed that these taxes were just and fair. Britain faced a massive debt following the French and Indian War, and much of the expense had involved protecting the colonies. It seemed right that the colonies should now carry some of the expense of the war through a few taxes.

The colonists did not agree. They already paid taxes to their colonial governments; why should they now be expected to pay additional taxes to Britain, especially since they had no representation in the British Parliament, no members in the House of Commons?

The conflict and the arguments grew louder. The colonists and the governing forces in England—Parliament and King George III—grew angry at each other. One person who tried to bring the two sides together, to reconcile them, was Benjamin Franklin.

COLONIAL PEACEMAKER

Born in Boston in 1706, Franklin was much older than Thomas Paine. Franklin had already accomplished what Paine wanted to do, making a life and a name for himself. In the early part of the 1770s, Franklin was in England, trying to bring Britain and the colonies together. Finally, though, he decided it could not be done. He decided this in the year 1774, and it was that same year that he met Thomas Paine.

Paine had left Thetford and gone to London. He hoped to make a life as a journalist there. He was finished with making clothes, and he was finished with collecting taxes. He wanted to make a living with words, with his pen.

Franklin and Paine met in the summer of 1774. Franklin was 68 years old. He was famous, he had money, and he was a successful printer and inventor. Paine was 37 years old. He had failed in most of the jobs he had held and he had no money. He had no one to recommend him or to help him.

For some reason (we'll never know exactly why), Benjamin Franklin decided to help Thomas Paine. Franklin suggested that Paine cross the great ocean and go to Philadelphia, which was where Franklin had made his own fortune. To help in this, Franklin wrote a letter recommending Paine. In it, Franklin said, "I request you to give him your best advice and countenance, as he is quite a stranger there. If you can put him in a way of obtaining employment as a clerk, or assistant tutor in a school, or assistant surveyor . . . you will do well."[6]

Armed only with a letter of introduction, Thomas Paine set forth across the great Atlantic Ocean.

Paine met Benjamin Franklin in London in the summer of 1774.
Franklin advised Paine to move to Philadelphia and wrote him
a letter of introduction.

Test Your Knowledge

1 Where was Thomas Paine born?

    a. Virginia.

    b. Massachusetts.

    c. New Jersey.

    d. England.

2 What was Paine's father's profession?

    a. Blacksmith.

    b. Sailor.

    c. Maker of stays.

    d. Doctor.

3 As a teenager, Paine was hired to do what?

    a. Collect taxes.

    b. Work as a clerk in a dry goods store.

    c. Serve as an apprentice to a shopkeeper.

    d. Teach.

4 Why did Paine travel to London?

    a. To collect taxes.

    b. To become a journalist.

    c. To visit his cousin.

    d. To collect fabric for his clothing business.

5 Which famous patriot met Paine in London and encouraged him to go to the American colonies?

a. Thomas Jefferson.

b. John Adams.

c. George Washington.

d. Benjamin Franklin.

ANSWERS: 1. d; 2. c; 3. a; 4. b; 5. d

The Newest American

Lurch. Boom. Splash. The ship *London Packet* dropped anchor at Philadelphia, the largest port in the American colonies. There were 120 passengers aboard, most of whom were in the steerage compartments. Only five or so well-to-do passengers had paid the higher price and received a cabin of their own.

In one of those cabins was Thomas Paine. He had arrived in Philadelphia, one of the most important of all the American cities. But Thomas Paine was too ill to rise from bed. He was even too ill to move about in bed. Anyone seeing him must have thought he would surely perish.

The *London Packet* had had a terrible voyage. Leaving England in October, the passengers had experienced an epidemic of fever, which was probably typhus. Some of the passengers had died. Many of those who survived were sick.

This was not the greeting Thomas Paine had hoped for, but it was the typical, rude arrival that happened to many who washed up on America's shore. Unless he got better, and quickly, there would soon be an end to his life story.

A Philadelphia doctor came on board the ship. He examined the sick people and took special care to look at Thomas Paine. The Englishman had a letter of recommendation from Philadelphia's most famous citizen, Benjamin Franklin. Words of praise from Franklin were usually heeded in Philadelphia. This was the city where Franklin had become famous as author of *Poor Richard's Almanac*. Franklin was now in

London, as the colonial representative to the British government. His letter said: "Thomas Paine is very well recommended to me as an ingenious worthy young man. He goes to Pennsylvania with a view of settling there. I request you to give him your best advice and countenance, as he is quite a stranger there. If you can put him in a way of obtaining employment as a clerk, assistant tutor in a school, or assistant surveyor, all of which I think him very capable . . . you will do well, and much oblige your affectionate father."[7]

The letter was addressed to Benjamin Franklin's son and also to his son-in-law. Both of them were important men, who, if they wished to, could do good things for the recently arrived Englishman.

The Philadelphia doctor took Thomas Paine ashore. The Englishman had to be carried out on a stretcher because of his illness. Soon he was resting at a place found for him by the good doctor.

Thomas Paine did not recover quickly. Typhus is a serious illness and many people died from it in the eighteenth century. But Thomas Paine had spent much of his life outdoors. He had been a tax collector, who had ridden on horseback over many long, lonely miles. This exercise now stood him well, for he began to

Paine's letter from Franklin ensured him a warm reception when he arrived in Philadelphia. Franklin was one of the most famous men in the colonies. He had long been a supporter of the movement for colonial unity, as illustrated in his *Join, or Die* print.

recover. The process lasted for about six weeks. By the beginning of the New Year, 1775, Thomas Paine was nearly well.

JOURNALIST IN PENNSYLVANIA

In the time that Thomas Paine lay in his sick bed, the American colonies edged closer to a complete break with England, their mother country. The Americans had called a Continental Congress, which met in Philadelphia in September 1774. While Thomas Paine was crossing the Atlantic on board the *London Packet*, the Continental Congress had decided to boycott all English goods. The boycott went into effect on December 1, 1774, precisely one day after Thomas Paine first came ashore.

Thomas Paine recovered by the start of the new year. He went for about a month without any work and, probably, without much to eat during that time. Then, he found work as a journalist with the new *Pennsylvania Magazine*.

The owner and editor of the magazine wanted this to be a truly American journal. He wanted the news to be of what happened in America and what Americans were doing. The owner was sad to see that most of the news focused on America's conflict with England.

Thomas Paine's first job in America was to answer letters sent to the editor. He did so using a saucy style that showed his English roots. One such answer was: "The verses signed a SUBSCRIBER are too imperfect for publication. We presume the author will think the same when his muse becomes a little calmer."[8]

Philadelphia in 1775

The American Revolution began in the spring of 1775. Because the Second Continental Congress was meeting in Philadelphia at that time, that city took on a special importance in the fight for freedom.

Philadelphia had been laid out by William Penn and his Quaker colonists in 1682. The city was designed with wide streets and avenues, allowing carts and wagons plenty of room in which to move goods. Philadelphia was designed, from the beginning, as a market and trade city. This meant that farmers brought in their produce and sold it in the streets, and that some articles were packed and shipped overseas. By 1775, Philadelphia was not only the largest town in the British colonies, but also the second largest town or city in the entire British Empire! Only London had more people.

Thomas Paine had the good fortune to land in Philadelphia, where so much was happening in 1775. It would have been bad luck had he landed in Charleston or New York City, since neither of them would have given him the same opportunities to speak and write in defense of American liberty.

In April 1775, just four months after arriving in America, Thomas Paine learned of the Battles of Lexington and Concord. On April 19, British troops went west from Boston. They went to the towns of Lexington and Concord, in the colony of Massachusetts, looking for American muskets, powder, and ball.

The colonists fought the British at Lexington and lost. Then they fought them at Concord, which was more of a draw. By the later afternoon, the British were headed back to Boston. As they went east, the British were shot at by hundreds, even thousands of colonists, who fired from behind the cover of trees and stone walls. By the time the British got back to Boston, they had suffered about 300 men killed, wounded, or missing.

Everyone could see that these two battles were the beginning of something very large. Thomas Paine, as a journalist for the *Pennsylvania Magazine*, wrote about a dream he had soon after he heard the news: "The beautiful country which you saw is America. The sickly state you beheld her in has been coming on her for these ten years past. Her commerce has been drying up by repeated restrictions, till by one merciless edict the ruin of it is completed. . . . The tempest is the present contest, and the main event will be the same. She will rise with new glories from the conflict, and her name will be established in every corner of the globe." [9]

This was an Englishman writing about America. How did he know so much?

This was a foreigner who had just arrived. How did he understand the American spirit so well?

Thomas Paine was a man without a country, but he had now adopted America for his own.

Test Your Knowledge

1 Paine left London and traveled to which American city?
- a. Boston.
- b. New York.
- c. Philadelphia.
- d. Williamsburg.

2 Paine carried a letter of introduction from Franklin. To whom was it addressed?
- a. A doctor who was one of Franklin's close friends.
- b. Thomas Jefferson.
- c. Samuel Adams.
- d. Franklin's son and son-in-law.

3 When Paine first arrived in America, he was suffering from what illness?
- a. Malaria.
- b. Typhus.
- c. Yellow fever.
- d. Appendicitis.

4 Where did Paine first find work?
- a. At an apothecary.
- b. At a courthouse.
- c. At the *Pennsylvania Magazine*.
- d. At an inn.

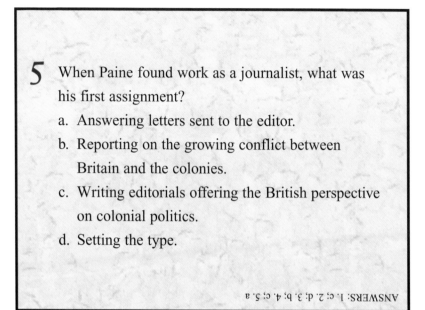

5 When Paine found work as a journalist, what was his first assignment?

a. Answering letters sent to the editor.

b. Reporting on the growing conflict between Britain and the colonies.

c. Writing editorials offering the British perspective on colonial politics.

d. Setting the type.

ANSWERS: 1. c; 2. d; 3. b; 4. c; 5. a

Declarations of Independence

The Revolutionary War had begun. The American militia-men now boxed the British in at Boston. There was a long, but not very active, siege of the city.

Philadelphia was the home of the Second Continental Congress. Its leaders were John Adams, Benjamin Franklin, Samuel Adams, John Hancock, and others. These men knew that the fight for independence had begun, but they still hoped something might be done to prevent an all-out war with England.

Thomas Paine began to meet prominent Americans at roundtable discussions. These informal talks paved the way for greater understanding among the American revolutionaries. Certainly one can ask: How did a British subject, recently arrived in America, get to participate in these talks?

The American Revolution was so young, so slow getting on its feet, that most American Patriots welcomed help, even if it came from someone so new to the colonies. No one seems to have minded that Thomas Paine took part in the discussions; some people even welcomed this because, as someone new to the conflict, he could give a different point of view.

COMMON SENSE

By the summer of 1775, Thomas Paine had broken with Thomas Aitkins, the publisher of the *Pennsylvania Magazine*. We are not quite sure of the reasons why, but Paine was often a difficult person with whom to work. He was vain about his writing, thought it very grand, and had a hard time accepting changes. Also, as he became more of a revolutionary, Thomas Paine became more outspoken in his views.

The autumn of 1775 brought fresh challenges for the American cause. American troops under Benedict Arnold invaded Canada, hoping to bring that British colony into a position of support for the Patriots. While Patriots waited for news from Canada, Thomas Paine took the opportunity to strike out on his own as a writer.

Up until that time, Thomas Paine had written articles to fulfill assignments. The only piece of truly original writing he had done had been *The Case of the Officers of the Excise*, published in England in 1772. Now he went off in a new, strikingly original direction. He wrote *Common Sense*, a 46-page pamphlet, published in Philadelphia in January of 1776.

Even centuries later, his words still have extraordinary power:

> Some writers have so confounded society with government, as to leave little or no distinction between them; whereas they are not only different, but have different origins. Society is produced by our wants, and government by our wickedness; the former

COMMON SENSE:

ADDRESSED TO THE

INHABITANTS

O F

A M E R I C A.

On the following interesting

S U B J E C T S.

I. Of the Origin and Design of Government in general, with concise Remarks on the English Constitution.

II. Of Monarchy and Hereditary Succession.

III. Thoughts on the present State of American Affairs.

IV. Of the present Ability of America, with some miscellaneous Reflections.

Written by an ENGLISHMAN.

By Thomas Paine

Man knows no Master save creating HEAVEN;
Or those whom choice and common good ordain.

THOMSON.

PHILADELPHIA, Printed

And Sold by R. BELL, in Third-Street, 1776.

Paine's *Common Sense* made a strong and clear argument for independence, inspiring many Americans to declare their support for the Patriot cause.

promotes our happiness *positively* by uniting our affections, the latter *negatively* by restraining our vices. The one encourages intercourse, the other creates distinctions. The first is a patron, the last a punisher.

Society in every state is a blessing, but government even in its best state is but a necessary evil in its worst state an intolerable one; for when we suffer, or are exposed to the same miseries by a government, which we might expect in a country without government, our calamities are heightened by reflecting that we furnish the means by which we suffer![10]

Even though the American Revolution had been under way for eight months, no one had used language like this before. Thomas Paine was bolder and more complete in his thinking than any Patriot who had yet come forth. He was arguing for the rights of Americans, to be sure, but he was also arguing for the rights of men and women everywhere.

Thomas Paine attacked the British system of government, which many people thought was the best in the world. A king, with a Parliament divided into the

House of Lords and the House of Commons, was seen as much better than what existed in other countries. But Thomas Paine went after the British system as if he were using a scalpel.

> Government by kings was first introduced into the world by the Heathens, from whom the children of Israel copied the custom. It was the most prosperous invention the Devil ever set on foot for the promotion of idolatry. The Heathens paid divine honors to their deceased kings, and the Christian world hath improved on the plan by doing the same to their living ones. How impious is the title of sacred majesty applied to a worm, who in the midst of his splendor is crumbling into dust![11]

Not satisfied with attacking the British monarchy, Thomas Paine went on to describe how much better independence was than the government that ruled in England. He then concluded with stirring words:

> In short, independence is the only bond that can tie and keep us together. . . . Let the names of Whig and Tory be extinct; and let none other be heard

among us, than those of a good citizen, an open and resolute friend, and a virtuous supporter of the Rights of Mankind and of the Free and Independent States of America.[12]

THE WORDS ECHO

Thomas Paine's *Common Sense* was printed in Philadelphia by Thomas Bell. Almost at once, the pamphlet began to sell out. First hundreds of copies were printed, then thousands. The demand for *Common Sense* increased throughout the winter of 1776.

Thomas Paine did not make much money from *Common Sense*. In his first arrangement with the printer, Thomas Paine asked that whatever money was due him should be used to buy warm winter clothing for the American troops in Canada. Then, as it became clear that *Common Sense* was a bestseller, Thomas Paine tried to gain more money from the printer. But by then it was too late. *Common Sense* was so successful, and was read by so many people, that printers could "pirate" it almost at will, and neither Thomas Paine nor the original printer ever received much money for their labor.

Did this matter? To Thomas Paine the man, yes.

Did this matter to Thomas Paine the Patriot? No.

Nearly everyone who cared about the independence movement read *Common Sense*. A few people (John Adams was one) thought that Paine had only expressed what others had already thought. But most readers believed that Thomas Paine had carried the day. His arguments for independence were so strong and so clearly written that thousands of Americans now declared themselves to be Patriots.

By the spring of 1776, thousands of people had read *Common Sense*. In June 1776, Richard Lee of Virginia rose on the floor of the Continental Congress. He put forth a resolution that the Congress should declare the colonies in rebellion were "free and independent states."

It would have been nice if Thomas Paine had been asked to write the new Declaration of Independence. But that honor went to Thomas Jefferson, a delegate from Virginia. Jefferson wrote his draft in about ten days, and after a few days of debate, Congress approved the Declaration of Independence on July 2, 1776. Thomas Paine was not present at the Continental Congress, but he had the satisfaction of knowing what he had done for the cause of liberty.

VOLUNTEER SOLDIER

As the delegates to the Continental Congress were calling for independence, the American cause reached its lowest ebb.

In the summer of 1776, the British landed a large army on Staten Island. The British won the Battle of Long Island in August and then captured New York City in September. George Washington and the Continental Army had to flee New York in haste.

Thomas Paine decided to join the Continental Army as a volunteer. He joined a company called the Flying Regiment, named because they "flew" to whatever scene or area where help was most needed. In the autumn of 1776, Thomas Paine was at Fort Washington, a fort defended by General Nathanael Greene.

Nathanael Greene was a Quaker from Rhode Island. Unlike most Quakers, he approved of fighting if the cause was just. Thomas Paine's father was a Quaker, and he and Nathanael Greene got along extremely well. They saw many things the same way.

General Greene decided to hold Fort Washington, on the west bank of the Hudson River. This went against orders, for General Washington had commanded Greene to retreat from the fort. But General Greene stuck to his position, and when the British and their German allies (the Hessians) attacked, General Greene was lucky to get away with his life. So was Thomas Paine, who marched with the defeated army through New Jersey.

As they approached the Delaware River, the American Patriots hit their lowest point. In the space of just four months, the British had defeated them time and time again, pushing them from New York City, from New York, and now across New Jersey. If the British had pressed home their attacks, the entire Revolution might have been over in a few days. George Washington wrote to his brother that, "If every nerve is not strained to recruit the new army with all possible expedition, I think the game is pretty near up."[13]

Thomas Paine went to Philadelphia. He was out of uniform and back in his more familiar role as a writer. Looking at the situation, he decided that only heroic measures could save the day. One December 19, 1776, he published the first issue of *The Crisis*, with its famous beginning: "THESE are the times that try men's souls."

(continued on page 44)

Crossing the Delaware

It is probably the most famous picture or image from American history. George Washington stands tall in a boat that crosses the ice-caked Delaware River. His men pull at the oars or guard their muskets from the flakes of snow and rain. This is the moment when the Americans took the offensive against the British and their Hessian allies.

How much of it is true?

We are quite certain that General George Washington and about 3,000 men crossed the Delaware River that night. We are certain that it was cold, and that the Americans who crossed suffered from the cold. Many of them had uniforms that were worn out from months of service. Some of them did not have proper shoes.

But did George Washington stand in the boat? Probably not.

Were the pieces of floating ice really that big or terrifying? Probably not.

Finally, does it matter?

Not in the sense that the crossing of the Delaware and the Battle of Trenton gave new life to the American cause. What had seemed desperate on the day before Christmas became possible, even hopeful, on the day after Christmas. This was the Christmas surprise, planned by George Washington, but also made possible by the writing of Thomas Paine.

The *American* CRISIS.

NUMBER I.

By the Author of COMMON SENSE.

THESE are the times that try men's souls: The summer soldier and the sunshine patriot will, in this crisis, shrink from the service of his country; but he that stands it NOW, deserves the love and thanks of man and woman. Tyranny, like hell, is not easily conquered; yet we have this consolation with us, that the harder the conflict, the more glorious the triumph. What we obtain too cheap, we esteem too lightly:—'Tis dearness only that gives every thing its value. Heaven knows how to set a proper price upon its goods; and it would be strange, indeed, if so celestial an article as FREEDOM should not be highly rated. Britain, with an army to enforce her tyranny, has declared, that she has a right (*not only to* TAX, but) "to " BIND *us in* ALL CASES WHATSOEVER," and if being *bound in that manner* is not slavery, then is there not such a thing as slavery upon earth. Even the expression is impious, for so unlimited a power can belong only to GOD.

WHETHER the Independence of the Continent was declared too soon, or delayed too long, I will not now enter into as an argument; my own simple opinion is, that had it been eight months earlier, it would have been much better. We did not make a proper use of last winter, neither could we, while we were in a dependent state. However, the fault, if it were one, was all our own; we have none to blame but ourselves *. But no great deal is lost yet; all that Howe has been doing for this month past is rather a ravage than a conquest, which the spirit of the Jersies a year ago would have quickly repulsed, and which time and a little resolution will soon recover.

I have as little superstition in me as any man living, but **my**

---

* ".. The present winter" (meaning the last) " is worth an " age if rightly employed, but if lost, or neglected, the whole " Continent will partake of the evil; and there is no punish- " ment that man does not deserve, be he who, or what, or " where he will, that may be the means of sacrificing a season " so precious and useful."   COMMON SENSE.

Paine's *The Crisis* contained the famous phrase, "These are the times that try men's souls."

(continued from page 41)

These words quickly became immortal. General George Washington had them read aloud to the troops who had endured the past four months. Fortified by these words, General Washington and the Continental Army re-crossed the Delaware River. This time they went as the attackers. They fought the Hessian troops at the Battle of Trenton and won a complete victory.

Seldom has the power of the printed word been so effective.

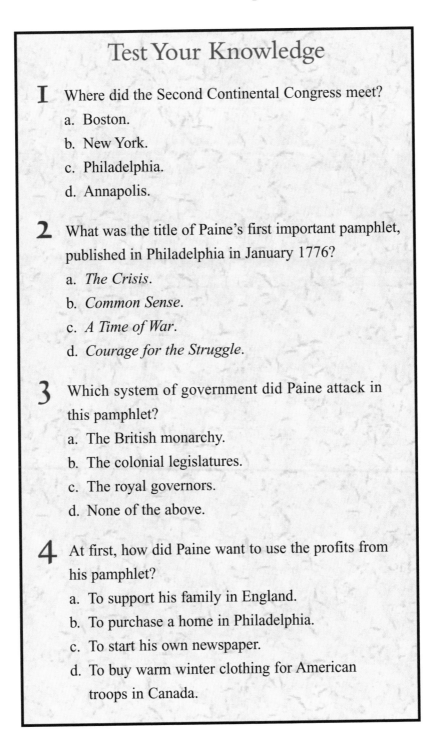

Test Your Knowledge

I Where did the Second Continental Congress meet?

a. Boston.

b. New York.

c. Philadelphia.

d. Annapolis.

2 What was the title of Paine's first important pamphlet, published in Philadelphia in January 1776?

a. *The Crisis*.

b. *Common Sense*.

c. *A Time of War*.

d. *Courage for the Struggle*.

3 Which system of government did Paine attack in this pamphlet?

a. The British monarchy.

b. The colonial legislatures.

c. The royal governors.

d. None of the above.

4 At first, how did Paine want to use the profits from his pamphlet?

a. To support his family in England.

b. To purchase a home in Philadelphia.

c. To start his own newspaper.

d. To buy warm winter clothing for American troops in Canada.

5 Which Patriot criticized Paine's writing as an expression of what others had already said?

a. Patrick Henry.

b. Benjamin Franklin.

c. Thomas Jefferson.

d. John Adams.

ANSWERS: 1. c; 2. b; 3. a; 4. d; 5. d

A Storm
of Troubles

Thomas Paine had now become famous, and was closely identified with the American fight for independence. He was the author of *Common Sense* and *The Crisis*, both of which were read by thousands of Americans.

It would be pleasant to say that Thomas Paine continued in this winning way, but it would be untrue. Instead,

Thomas Paine now entered a long period of conflict and setbacks.

Things started off well enough. In January 1777, Thomas Paine was sent as secretary to a group of delegates from the Continental Congress. The delegates went to meet chiefs of the Six Nations of Iroquois, who lived in upstate New York. Thomas Paine met many of the Indian leaders, and introduced himself to each one of them as "Common Sense."

In the winter of 1777, the Continental Congress voted to make Thomas Paine secretary to the committee on foreign affairs. This was a small but important post, and Thomas Paine cherished the memory of that honor for the rest of his life.

While the year had begun with good things for Thomas Paine, the same could not be said for the young United States. George Washington had won the Battle of Trenton, it is true, but he and his American troops were still greatly outnumbered. In the spring and summer of 1777, the British put together a three-pronged offensive intended to win the war with a knockout blow.

One army, led by General Burgoyne, was to come south from Canada. A second was to leave

In 1777, the Continental Congress voted to appoint Paine to the post of secretary to the committee on foreign affairs.

Canada and come south by way of Lake Ontario. A third army was to leave New York City and drive straight north. All three armies were to meet at Albany, New York. By holding that town and the entire length of the Hudson River, they could split the rebellious colonies (which now called themselves states) in two.

Thomas Paine was not a soldier. Even though he had participated in the last part of the campaign of 1776, he was much handier with his pen than a musket. Now, in his position as secretary to the committee on foreign affairs, he had a chance to make a difference.

All during 1777, while the British launched their attacks, the American committee on foreign affairs was hoping for a new alliance with France. True, France had always been an enemy of the American colonies, so long as they were part of the British Empire. But now, with the Americans fighting England, they hoped to win France to their side.

Thomas Paine had to re-think some of his own opinions. In *Common Sense,* he had argued against any foreign alliances, saying that the Americans would do best to win independence by their own efforts. But he could see, in 1777, that help was needed.

Luckily for the Americans, the British tripped over their own plans. One army did come south from Canada, but the one coming by way of Lake Ontario was tricked into retreat (the ruse was pulled by General Benedict Arnold). The third army, based in New York City, turned and went in another direction entirely. The British general, William Howe, took his army by sea to Chesapeake Bay, landed his men, and marched toward Philadelphia.

Philadelphia was the largest city in the colonies. This city had been the seat of both the First and the Second Continental Congress. Many people believed that if the British captured this city, the American cause would collapse.

Thomas Paine did not think so. He had never been impressed with cities as the center of American strength. Both in *Common Sense* and in later writings, he emphasized that the strength of America was that it was a *continent*—a landmass that could not easily be conquered, as long as there was free room to stand.

Even so, Thomas Paine knew that this was a dangerous time. When George Washington and the American army were defeated at the Battle of Brandywine Creek, Thomas Paine tried to encourage the people of Philadelphia to fortify the city and resist. His efforts were of no use. The people panicked. Many of them fled the city, and Thomas Paine had no choice but to run, as well. The author of *Common Sense* and *The Crisis* packed his bags yet again, and escaped to the countryside.

WINTER OF DISCONTENT

Thomas Paine traveled to one of the camps of the Continental Army. He arrived in time to see the last part of the Battle of Germantown. General Washington had attacked the British and caught them by surprise. The Americans were doing very well that morning, until some of their units collided in a dense patch of fog. Americans fired on Americans, causing casualties. Soon, the Continental Army was in full retreat.

General Washington was upset, because he knew how close he had come to winning a victory. Many Americans were discouraged and full of despair over the cause of independence. As doubt and gloom surrounded the cause for independence, General Washington took his troops into winter quarters at Valley Forge, Pennsylvania.

Thomas Paine did not spend the cold winter of 1778 at Valley Forge. First, he stayed with friends, and then he joined the Continental Congress at its new home, in York, Pennsylvania. Thomas Paine did not have much money, but he was such an engaging conversationalist and had so much to say that he was a welcome guest and had many friends willing to offer him hospitality.

During the winter of 1778, American ambassadors persuaded France to sign two treaties with the United States, one of military alliance and another of commercial interests. Thomas Paine was happy to hear the news, even though he had previously written against alliances of any kind. He understood that France's support was vital to ensure that the fight for liberty could continue.

Finally, as winter drew to an end, the British decided to evacuate Philadelphia. They left in the spring of 1778, and many who had fled the city, including Thomas Paine, now felt safe to return.

THE SILAS DEANE AFFAIR

This might have been a wonderful time for Thomas Paine. The new alliance with France promised great things. The war seemed as if it might be won quickly.

But Thomas Paine, who was never shy about promoting his opinion or launching into a fiery argument, fell into a trap of his own making. He was the first person to denounce Silas Deane.

The "Silas Deane Affair" is one of the most perplexing cases of the American Revolution. Silas Deane was a Connecticut merchant who went to France in 1776 and arranged for guns, powder, and ammunition to be sent to America. The French government provided the weapons but sent them through a "dummy" (or fake) place of business. All seemed well until Thomas Paine took up his pen and attacked Silas Deane.

Deane, he wrote, was taking profits from the business transactions. This was not a crime, but it was unpatriotic.

That was all Thomas Paine said. But it was enough to set the city of Philadelphia on edge.

Members of the Continental Congress soon became divided into pro-Deane and anti-Deane factions. Many people blamed Thomas Paine for having caused the trouble. On one occasion, he was tripped by an officer of the Continental Army and fell into a sewer.

Worse still, Paine was attacked by the new French ambassador to America. Thomas Paine, the ambassador

Paine's critique of Silas Deane cost him his congressional post and made him the subject of attacks like this political cartoon, in which Paine dreams of ghosts ready to take him to the gallows and stocks for his writings.

wrote, had attacked the honor of France by suggesting that extra profits had been made. Because the new alliance with France was of great importance, the Continental Congress put aside all other business for a while and concentrated on the accusations made by Thomas Paine against Silas Deane.

Thomas Paine would not back down. He offered his resignation as secretary to the committee on foreign affairs, but he would not take back one word he had written on the Silas Deane matter. Once, the Continental Congress refused to accept his resignation. Then the matter arose again, and this time his resignation was accepted. He was paid $250 in back pay and asked to retire from his official duties.

Silas Deane and other Businessmen

We tend to forget that business—the exchange of money and goods—goes on in almost every season and every time of life. Times of war are no exception. Businessmen still act to gain profits.

Thomas Paine had a deep distrust of businessmen. The ones he had known in England had kept him poor. The ones he knew in America he did not like. Even the most patriotic of these businessmen were, to Thomas Paine, a little suspicious.

Silas Deane was one of a number of businessmen who served the American cause. Two other prominent ones were Robert Morris of Pennsylvania and Gouverneur Morris of New York (The two men were not related). Thomas Paine tangled with both men at

All this does not seem so bad. Thomas Paine was still the author of *The Crisis*. He was one of the best known of all the American revolutionaries. But he was still, in many ways, a man without a country. Some Patriots, especially in the Continental Congress, still described him as an English adventurer, someone who did not really belong. Things got so bad that Thomas Paine began to talk about leaving America.

different times. Gouverneur Morris used harsh language against Thomas Paine at the time when the Continental Congress fired him as secretary for foreign affairs. Robert Morris was more temperate in his judgments, but he and Thomas Paine disagreed on many issues. By the time the Revolutionary War ended in 1783, the merchants seemed to have gained the upper hand, both in the Continental Congress and in the country as a whole. Not until much later was it found that Silas Deane had indeed made illegal profits and that he had started a correspondence with Great Britain over how to end the war. This does not blacken the name of his many business associates, but it gives some support to Thomas Paine's early condemnation of Silas Deane.

Test Your Knowledge

I In January 1777, Paine was sent as secretary to a congressional delegation meeting with whom?

  a. A group of British generals.

  b. Representatives from France.

  c. Washington and his military advisors.

  d. Chiefs of the Six Nations of Iroquois.

2 After this mission, Paine was appointed secretary to a congressional committee. Which one?

  a. The committee on foreign affairs.

  b. The committee on war.

  c. The committee on appropriations.

  d. The committee on public relations.

3 In 1777, the Continental Congress hoped for an alliance with which country?

  a. Spain.

  b. France.

  c. Germany.

  d. Scotland.

4 After the British captured Philadelphia, where did the Continental Congress meet?

  a. Valley Forge, Pennsylvania.

  b. Trenton, New Jersey.

  c. York, Pennsylvania.

  d. Easton, Pennsylvania.

5 Thomas Paine was attacked for his criticism of which businessman?

a. John Hancock.

b. George Wythe.

c. Silas Deane.

d. Paul Revere.

ANSWERS: 1. d; 2. a; 3. b; 4. c; 5. c

OUR RIGHTS AND OUR LIBERTIES

Sweet Victory

One of the lowest times in the life of Thomas Paine
came in 1779. He felt rejected and unappreciated.
He had obtained another job, this time serving as
secretary to the Pennsylvania legislature. But this job
was mostly clerical and gave little scope for his great
literary talents.

Thomas Paine yearned for something new, a fresh start. He seriously considered going back to England, to work for the American Patriot cause while in England. Friends talked him out of this idea, convincing him that he would end up arrested and hanged for treason.

Surprisingly, Thomas Paine found his next cause in the area of paper money. He had never been good at figures or business. Money had a way of slipping through his fingers, and he often had to be taken in by friends because he could not pay his own rent. But all these mishaps with money may have led Thomas Paine to his new subject: the debate over paper currency and hard money, meaning silver or gold.

Whether he worked for the Continental Congress or the legislature of Pennsylvania, Thomas Paine was paid in Continental paper money. Because the United States was a new nation, and because it did not have reserves of gold or silver, the paper notes were accepted by merchants at a lower and lower value. Sometimes an entire Continental dollar was accepted for an item costing only one copper penny, and the expression "Not worth a Continental" entered the English language.

Thomas Paine cared deeply about this matter. The matter was personal to him because of the paper script he received as his pay. So, in 1780, he brought out another major pamphlet. This one was entitled *Public Good*.

Public Good was concerned with the public lands to the west. Some states, like Virginia, claimed that the western lands belonged to them, arguing that the boundaries of their state stretched as far west as the Pacific Ocean! This idea had come about from the charters the British government had originally given the settlers. But, as Thomas Paine pointed out, those charters were no longer the law of the land. The Articles of Confederation, which were drawn up by the Continental Congress, were now the law of the United States.

Thomas Paine had written about bigger and more important issues before. If he had not written *Common Sense* and *The Crisis*, the young nation might not have lived through its first two years. But nothing he had written brought him as much criticism as *Public Good*.

Virginians were the most upset by Paine's pamphlet. Old friends, like Richard Henry Lee, never spoke in favor of Thomas Paine again. Others, like George Washington, accepted Paine's argument cautiously, but their suspicions of Paine grew. He was becoming less popular in the land he had done so much to help.

Things got so bad that Thomas Paine was eager to leave America. He had been there for six years and thought he had done all that he could. Now he was ready to return to England, or to some other part of Europe.

TRAVEL TO FRANCE

Paine's chance came in the autumn of 1780. The American cause was in a very bad way. Troops had gone for months without any pay. Some of the troops had very poor clothing and quarters. In this crisis, the Continental Congress decided to send Colonel John Laurens as a special ambassador to France, to ask for financial aid.

Thomas Paine knew Colonel Laurens well. Laurens asked the Continental Congress to make Thomas Paine his official secretary for the journey. This would be an important, paid job, but the Congress turned down the request. Thomas Paine had made many enemies by

In 1780, Paine left America to travel to France. His writing in *Public Good* had cost him the support of many friends.

now, and it was harder than ever for him to gain any type of paid work.

Paine found a way around the situation. He told Colonel Laurens that he would be willing to go as an unpaid "friend," accompanying Laurens on the voyage. As it turned out, Colonel Laurens did find another secretary, who was approved by Congress, and all three men went north to Boston, where they boarded the ship *Alliance*, headed for France.

Thomas Paine had taken one transatlantic voyage before, in the autumn of 1774. He well remembered how many of the crew and passengers had fallen sick, and how he had barely come through the ordeal. But such was his desire to leave America, and to spend time in France, that he braved the voyage.

There was a bad week when the ship had to fight her way through the ice. Then there were narrow scrapes with British warships in the Atlantic. But finally, to Paine's great relief, the ship touched land in one of the harbors of western France. Thomas Paine was back in Europe, for the first time in six years.

Colonel Laurens and Thomas Paine went to Paris, where they were met by Benjamin Franklin. He and Paine had not seen each other in some time, and the two men were both struck by how much had taken place since their last meeting. Benjamin Franklin had done great things in France. He had won the affection of the Parisians with his simple manners and homespun clothing. He had helped to bring about the two treaties of alliance between France and the United States, signed in 1778. But now it remained to be seen whether France and the United States could win the war.

Transatlantic Voyages

Today, in the twenty-first century, a transatlantic voyage is not a major process. People can fly in airplanes over the Atlantic in only six hours, while freighters and passenger ships often take a week to make the same crossing. Needless to say, it was much more difficult to cross the Atlantic Ocean in the eighteenth century.

Thomas Paine crossed the Atlantic five times in his life. This was far more than most people did; there were many people who never even crossed the ocean once.

Thomas Paine, like other passengers, found that the voyage was very unpredictable. If you had good winds and fair skies, you could cross from Boston to London in about four weeks. But if you had poor winds and sullen skies, the same voyage could take eight or nine weeks.

Things were in a bad way for the Franco-American cause. The French government was weary of sending what seemed like endless sums of money to help the Americans. The American government thought, rightly, that France cared more about damaging England than it did of helping the United States. At times like these, alliances tend to break down, and it was John Laurens's job to keep this one together.

Major storms, like hurricanes, could add weeks more to the schedule.

While hurricanes posed a special threat, ship captains were as fearful of being "becalmed." This meant you had no wind to fill your sails and your ship stayed just about where it was, with the empty sails flapping quietly. Being becalmed was dangerous in its own way, because your ship drifted with the tide, sometimes in directions that you really did not want to go.

Crossing the Atlantic Ocean remained a major task until the creation of the first steamships in the nineteenth century. Then, for the first time, ships could move at a constant speed, regardless of which way the winds blew.

Journeys across the Atlantic were long and dangerous during the eighteenth century, as shown in this illustration. Ships were dependent on the wind, and rough seas could lengthen the journey by several weeks.

Thomas Paine had no official standing in the United States delegation. He was merely a friend of Colonel John Laurens. What was more, Thomas Paine spoke almost no French. Embarrassed by this, he stayed in his hotel room most of the time, and was little help to Colonel Laurens. Laurens made some mistakes. On one occasion, he went straight up to King Louis XVI at a court function and tried to tell him how much the Americans needed financial assistance. This was simply not done. It was considered poor manners. That kind of business was meant for ambassadors and ministers.

Despite these setbacks, good news came early in the summer of 1781. Not only did France approve a major loan to the United States, but a French fleet in the Caribbean intended to sail north to help the Americans fight the British. Satisfied with this development, Colonel John Laurens and Thomas Paine sailed back to America, after having spent only five months in France.

RETURN TO AMERICA

The return voyage was much longer and harder. The ship took nearly 80 days to sail from France to Boston, and by the time he got off the ship, Thomas Paine vowed never to travel by sea again (a vow he would have to break).

Once off the boat, Thomas Paine and John Laurens set out for Philadelphia. They had with them a number of wagons that carried the gold that France had lent to the United States. At one point on the journey, John Laurens had to hasten on ahead, leaving Thomas Paine behind. Paine made it to New York City, and then to Philadelphia, feeling as if he had been treated badly by his friend.

Then came the best news in years. The French fleet had sailed from the Caribbean and anchored off the Virginia coast. Learning this, General George Washington marched most of the Continental Army south to Virginia. They joined with the French and trapped a major British army at a small village called Yorktown. In October 1781, General Charles Cornwallis surrendered his entire British army to the Franco-American forces. Although the war was not quite over, it was clear that the Americans had triumphed.

Thomas Paine was elated. But the great victory at Yorktown also left him rather at loose ends. What was he to do now?

Test Your Knowledge

1 After leaving his post with the Continental Congress, Paine was hired by which governmental organization?

a. The British Parliament.

b. The Pennsylvania legislature.

c. The Virginia House of Burgesses.

d. The Philadelphia Council.

2 What was the focus of Paine's *Public Good*?

a. The public lands to the west.

b. The alliance with France.

c. The need for independence from Britain.

d. None of the above.

3 In 1780, Paine left America to travel to which country?

a. Holland.

b. Britain.

c. France.

d. Italy.

4 After crossing the Atlantic Ocean, Paine met with which famous American?

a. Benjamin Franklin.

b. Thomas Jefferson.

c. John Adams.

d. Benedict Arnold.

5   When Thomas Paine and John Laurens returned to Philadelphia, what did they bring with them?

a. A fleet of French ships to be used by the American navy.

b. Gold that France had lent to the United States.

c. Copies of the signed alliance.

d. New uniforms for the Continental soldiers.

ANSWERS: 1. b; 2. a; 3. c; 4. a; 5. b

OUR RIGHTS AND OUR LIBERTIES

England
and France

The American Revolution was over. The colonists had won their independence. Thomas Paine celebrated along with all the others. He was overjoyed to see American independence become a reality.

But there was still work to do. Independence had been won, but a nation with a strong foundation still had to be made.

Thomas Paine was less suited to this kind of work. One of his greatest critics, John Adams, had written that Thomas Paine was better at tearing things down than at building them up. Thomas Paine knew this about himself. He was eager to go to other lands, other countries, where he might make more of a difference. But events kept him in America for a little while longer.

By 1782, Thomas Paine was in desperate need of money. He wrote a long letter to General George Washington, asking for some way in which the new nation might employ his talents. George Washington agreed to help him. He arranged for Thomas Paine to be hired by Congress to write pamphlets and papers in support of the new government, and to receive about $800 a year for this service.

One could argue that Thomas Paine was "bought" by this job, but it also fit right in with what he liked to do. He believed in a strong government, one with a sound currency and system of trade. All this was in his own mind, so he did not mind hiring out his pen to the Continental Congress. Knowing that many members of the Congress did not like Paine, Washington arranged for Paine to be paid from a secret account, one that the congressmen knew nothing about.

To fulfill his new job, Thomas Paine had to work closely with two men from the past. Robert Morris was a prominent businessman, with whom Paine had argued during the Silas Deane Affair. Gouverneur Morris was another businessman, and he had led the way in calling for Thomas Paine to be removed from his post as secretary to Congress for the committee on foreign affairs.

Surprisingly, Thomas Paine worked rather well with these two men. He knew they looked down on him as a foreigner and as an adventurer, but he came to respect them more and to see things more in the light that they did. In 1786, he brought out a pamphlet about the virtues of "hard" as opposed to "soft" money. Hard money meant pieces of copper, silver, or gold, while soft money meant paper currency that could be inflated or debased depending on what the government did.

By 1786, Thomas Paine had proved himself valuable to the American cause for a second or third time. Not only had he written the great revolutionary pamphlets of the 1770s, but he now turned out more conservative pamphlets, focusing on building a new nation.

At the same time, Thomas Paine also used his pen in his own service. He had gone through the Revolutionary War with little to show for it. Now, he petitioned both the Continental Congress and the states of Pennsylvania and New York for funds. He wanted to have enough money to buy land, and he wanted to become a respectable American citizen.

There was plenty of resistance to the requests. Many enemies of Thomas Paine made it difficult for these requests to be fulfilled. But, in the end, the Continental Congress gave him a small pension, and the state of New York granted him a section of land in what is now called New Rochelle, close to New York City. Thomas Paine had now fulfilled most of his ambitions. He had money, property, and his fame and name were now secure.

Yet he did not stay where he was. Thomas Paine seldom did.

ENGINEER IN ENGLAND

In 1787, he sailed from New York, headed for London. This was his fourth transatlantic voyage.

Peace now reigned between England, France, and the United States. There were no British warships lurking on the seas, and no enemy to threaten the safety of the voyage.

Thomas Paine arrived in England and went straight to London. He does not seem to have thought that some people would regard him as a traitor to England. Rather, he thought they would be interested in his scientific ideas and pursuits.

Thomas Paine had always been interested in engineering. He had long kept in his mind an idea for a bridge, made of iron and employing unusual arches to support its weight. He had never found anyone to back his cause in America. He hoped someone would do so in England.

Paine split his time between England and France. He was known in both countries, although he was most likely more popular in France than in England. But he never learned to speak French very well, so there were times when he was much happier in his homeland. Dividing his time between these two countries, Paine was at the right place as the second great revolution of his lifetime began.

A NEW REVOLUTION

The French Revolution began in the summer of 1789.

Paine was in England when the French Revolution began in 1789. His friend Thomas Jefferson was in Paris, and wrote to Paine with details of events like the storming of the Bastille.

Thomas Paine was in England that summer, but he was able to follow all the news and developments. What unfolded was truly amazing.

When France signed treaties of alliance with the United States, France was an absolute monarchy. This meant that the French king, Louis XVI, controlled the entire government. There were cabinet officials, secretaries, and ambassadors, of course, but the king was the absolute ruler.

France had been an absolute monarchy for so long that no one thought a revolution would happen there. If the idea of popular revolutions were to spread from America, like a sickness or a virus, then most believed it more likely to pop up in England or in Holland. Those countries had longer traditions of popular government. But it happened in France, in the summer of 1789.

Thomas Paine had lost the friendship of many Americans, but he still kept in touch with Thomas Jefferson. The Virginian was in Paris in 1789 and he and Thomas Paine kept up a lively correspondence about what was happening.

First, Parisian citizens attacked the Bastille. This was an old fort, in the center of the city, which had been turned into a prison. The people attacked, captured it, and killed the governor of the prison. All the prisoners were then freed.

Then the legislature, which had been summoned by King Louis, renamed itself the National Assembly. The delegates swore an oath in a tennis court (the Tennis Court Oath). They swore not to leave their posts until they had written and approved a new constitution for France.

Then, peasants in the countryside turned against the noblemen who owned most of the nation's land. The peasants attacked castles and manor houses in the countryside, often burning them to the ground.

King Louis XVI and Queen Marie Antoinette

He was French. She was Austrian. Their marriage was arranged by their families. She came from Austria in 1774, the same year that Thomas Paine first left England for America.

King Louis XVI was a good but dull man. He was not fit to be a king, a fact that he might even have admitted. He was a good husband and father and a rather good locksmith, but very uninterested in the business of governing his country.

Queen Marie Antoinette was different. She was sharp, smart, and calculating. She was a very beautiful woman, and all the ladies at court tried to imitate her. Queen Marie Antoinette would probably have made a better ruler than her good-natured husband.

When the French Revolution began in 1789, Marie Antoinette urged her husband to be stronger, to use force to put down the revolution. He usually took a long time to make any kind of decision, and by the time

No one knew quite what to make of the French Revolution. It was a frightening time, particularly for the wealthy, but there was also a sense of hope and optimism in the air—a sense that injustice could be

he agreed with her, it was too late. The revolution had grown too strong.

Both the king and the queen occasionally said silly or stupid things, demonstrating their lack of understanding of the lives of the people over whom they ruled. The most infamous occasion was when Queen Marie Antoinette asked one of her courtiers why the French people were unhappy. "Because they have no bread," was his answer. She gave a reply that has been remembered ever since, "Why, then let them eat cake."

No one knows whether she was being cruel or whether she was really that ignorant of the lives of the people. In either case, she will be forever remembered for this remark, and it is one of the reasons she and her husband are usually considered poor rulers, ill prepared to face the winds of change that swept over France as the eighteenth century ended.

brought to an end, that the independence and equality that Americans had achieved might also be achieved in France.

Thomas Paine was very pleased with what he heard. To him, it seemed as if the French Revolution was the perfect continuation of the American Revolution. The cause of liberty had never been stronger, at least in his eyes.

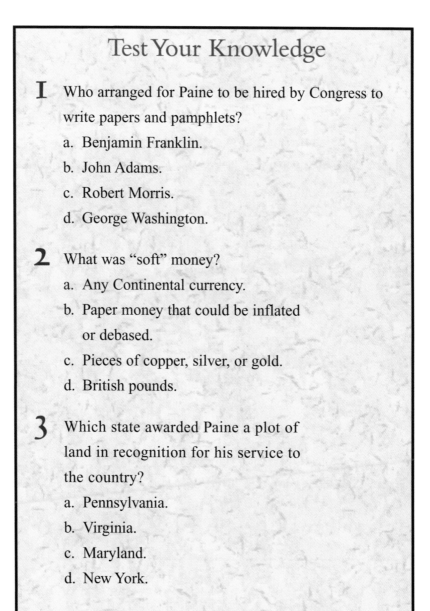

Test Your Knowledge

I Who arranged for Paine to be hired by Congress to write papers and pamphlets?

a. Benjamin Franklin.

b. John Adams.

c. Robert Morris.

d. George Washington.

2 What was "soft" money?

a. Any Continental currency.

b. Paper money that could be inflated or debased.

c. Pieces of copper, silver, or gold.

d. British pounds.

3 Which state awarded Paine a plot of land in recognition for his service to the country?

a. Pennsylvania.

b. Virginia.

c. Maryland.

d. New York.

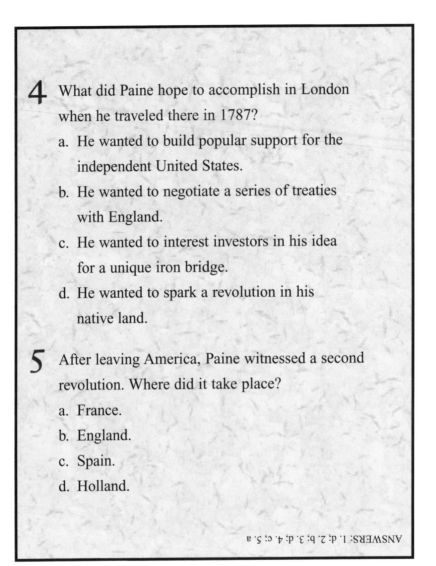

4 What did Paine hope to accomplish in London when he traveled there in 1787?

a. He wanted to build popular support for the independent United States.

b. He wanted to negotiate a series of treaties with England.

c. He wanted to interest investors in his idea for a unique iron bridge.

d. He wanted to spark a revolution in his native land.

5 After leaving America, Paine witnessed a second revolution. Where did it take place?

a. France.

b. England.

c. Spain.

d. Holland.

ANSWERS: 1. d; 2. b; 3. d; 4. c; 5. a

The Rights
of Man

Thomas Paine was in London in 1789. He knew about the events in Paris, but he was not a personal witness to the revolution at its beginning.

Someone whom Paine knew well was in Paris that year. This was Gouverneur Morris, the American merchant with whom Thomas Paine had worked in 1782 and 1783.

Thomas Paine was a strong supporter of the French Revolution. He thought it was wonderful that the spirit of liberty, born in America, had now spread to France.

Gouverneur Morris had a great distrust of the French Revolution. Morris believed that the American Revolution had been successful because men of property and education had led the way. What he saw in Paris led him to believe that the French Revolution would be very different.

Events turned in the year 1790. Louis XVI was still king, but he was now a monarch whose power was limited. France now had an independent legislature, the National Assembly.

The French revolutionaries took aim at the Catholic Church. Priests and bishops were required to swear allegiance to the new French government. This went against thousands of years of Catholic tradition, and many priests refused to swear allegiance to any political authority. As a result, the new French government made an enemy of the Catholic Church.

Thomas Paine was still in England in 1790 and 1791. He was still an observer of the events rather than a participant.

In 1790, the British philosopher Edmund Burke brought out an important new book. *Some Reflections on the Late Revolution in France* condemned many aspects of the French Revolution. Edmund Burke practically accused the French revolutionaries of destroying what they claimed to want to create. By getting rid of the important support of the Catholic Church and by taking land from the nobles, the revolutionaries were undermining the country itself.

Thomas Paine and Edmund Burke had been friends. Burke had introduced Paine to many leaders in Parliament and the two men had thought alike in the past. Thomas Paine took Edmund Burke's new book, and its critique of revolutionary behavior, as a personal attack, which it was not.

THE RIGHTS OF MAN

During 1791, Thomas Paine worked on his answer to Edmund Burke. As he researched and wrote in London, things got steadily worse in France.

King Louis XVI and Queen Marie Antoinette pretended to go along with the revolution. Secretly, though, they wrote to their relatives, the leaders of

In *The Rights of Man*, Paine showed his support for the French revolution in writing critical of King Louis XVI and monarchies. He was forced to flee to France when the British government threatened him with arrest.

Austria and Prussia, asking them to invade France and bring the revolution to an end.

Meanwhile, the French Revolutionaries continued to separate church and state. They continued to chip away at the ancient privileges of the noble class. From his place in London, just 150 miles away, Thomas Paine thought this was wonderful. Late in 1791, he brought out the first edition of his *The Rights of Man*.

No one really should have been surprised. *The Rights of Man* said the same things Thomas Paine had said in *Common Sense* and other publications. However, this time Paine wrote for a European audience. His readers were either thrilled or appalled by what they read, depending upon their views of the events in France.

In *The Rights of Man*, Paine attacked Burke and governments dependent upon the rule of a king:

'We have seen,' says Mr. Burke, 'the French rebel against a mild and lawful monarch, with more fury, outrage, and insult, than any people has been known to rise against the most illegal usurper, or the most sanguinary tyrant.' This is one among a thousand other instances, in which Mr. Burke shows that he is ignorant of the springs and principles of the French Revolution.

It was not against Louis XVI, but against the despotic principles of the Government, that the nation revolted. These principles had not their origin in him, but in the original establishment, many centuries back: and they were become too deeply rooted to be removed, and the Augean stables of parasites and plunderers too abominably filthy to be cleansed by anything short of a complete and universal Revolution. When it becomes necessary to do anything, the whole heart and soul should go into the measure, or not attempt it. That crisis was then arrived, and there remained no choice but to act with determined vigor, or not to act at all. The king was known to be the friend of the nation, and this circumstance was favorable to the enterprise. Perhaps no man bred up in the style of an absolute king, ever possessed a heart so little disposed to the exercise of that species of power as the present King of France. But the principles of the Government itself still remained the same. The Monarch and the Monarchy were distinct and separate things; and it was against the established despotism of the latter, and not against the person or principles of the former, that the revolt commenced, and the Revolution has been carried.[14]

Thomas Paine went on to argue that all the "rights of man" were his rights regardless of whether his parents or grandparents had been able to enforce them. It did not matter, Paine declared, whether one's ancestors had been oppressed or lost their rights. Those rights still belonged to their descendants, and to all people.

Thomas Jefferson had said much the same thing in the Declaration of Independence of 1776. But Thomas Paine wrote for a wider, international audience. Many people were pleased, even delighted, with what they read. Many others were horrified. They denounced Thomas Paine as a wild man, a radical, and slightly insane.

A HERO AND A THREAT

For the next eight or nine months, Thomas Paine lived in danger of arrest. The British government of King George III was unsure how to move against Paine, but they certainly wanted to. They interpreted his criticism of the French king as criticism of all kings.

Thomas Paine stayed out of London that spring and summer. He lived south of London, not far from the English Channel. Even so, he did not seem aware of the danger that threatened him. When friends urged him to leave England, either for France or for America, he hesitated. Paine was happy to be back in England, after so many years, and he did not want to take flight yet again.

But the time came when he had little choice. In September 1792, Thomas Paine learned two things. First, he had been elected a member of the National Convention, the new legislature in France. This honor had come to him without his seeking it. He had not run for office or asked for the post. But it was there for the taking.

Second, Thomas Paine learned he was about to be arrested for sedition. This meant that the British government had ruled that *The Rights of Man* was both wrong and against the government.

Learning this, Thomas Paine finally fled. He rushed to Dover, on the English side of the Channel. He was nearly arrested at the last minute, but he managed to get on a ferry headed for Calais in France.

As he crossed the beautiful waters that separate England from France, Thomas Paine may have looked back with sadness. England, the land of his birth, had never claimed him as the hero he thought he was. Instead it had forced him into exile.

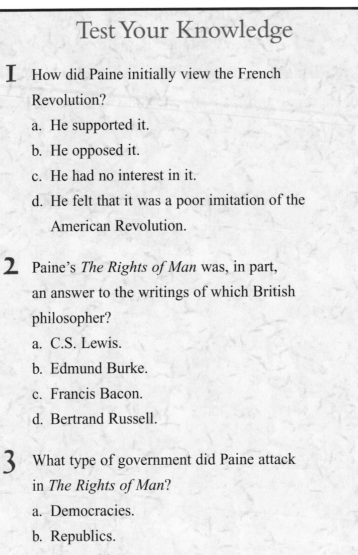

Test Your Knowledge

I How did Paine initially view the French
Revolution?
   a. He supported it.
   b. He opposed it.
   c. He had no interest in it.
   d. He felt that it was a poor imitation of the
      American Revolution.

2 Paine's *The Rights of Man* was, in part,
an answer to the writings of which British
philosopher?
   a. C.S. Lewis.
   b. Edmund Burke.
   c. Francis Bacon.
   d. Bertrand Russell.

3 What type of government did Paine attack
in *The Rights of Man*?
   a. Democracies.
   b. Republics.
   c. Monarchies.
   d. None of the above.

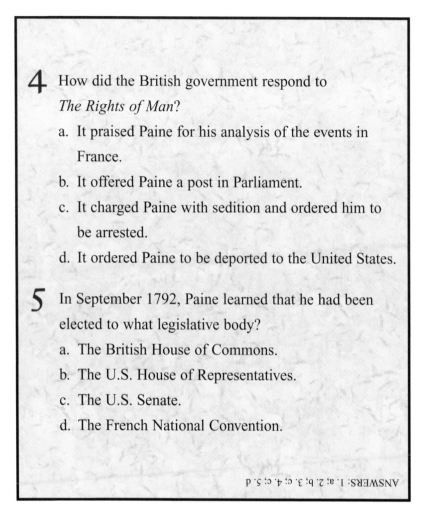

4 How did the British government respond to
The Rights of Man?

  a. It praised Paine for his analysis of the events in
     France.

  b. It offered Paine a post in Parliament.

  c. It charged Paine with sedition and ordered him to
     be arrested.

  d. It ordered Paine to be deported to the United States.

5 In September 1792, Paine learned that he had been
elected to what legislative body?

  a. The British House of Commons.

  b. The U.S. House of Representatives.

  c. The U.S. Senate.

  d. The French National Convention.

ANSWERS: 1. a; 2. b; 3. c; 4. c; 5. d

Prison and
Its Terrors

Thomas Paine landed at Calais, on the French side of the Channel. He was greeted by a band, by well-wishers, and by people who begged him to be their new representative in the National Convention. The French celebrated his arrival, and treated him as a patriot and hero.

Thomas Paine had been in exile before. He had faced hard times before. But never before had he been honored in this way, with an elected seat to a legislature. Naturally, he accepted the position.

Just a week or two later he was in Paris, being introduced to the other members of the National Convention. There were men there who had done great things, and others responsible for some of the bloodiest acts of the French Revolution. Paine found himself introduced to men like Danton, Marat, and Robespierre. One French leader was missing: the Marquis de Lafayette.

In the early days of the French Revolution, Lafayette had been a great hero. He had been the leader of the National Guard, and thousands of men had followed him in swearing allegiance to the new government. That ceremony had been held on the Field of Mars, in Paris, near where the Eiffel Tower stands today.

Lafayette had fallen on hard times. He was not conservative enough to keep the support of the nobles, his own class. He was not radical enough to win the support of the people of Paris, and his ties to the wealthy, noble class made many revolutionaries suspicious. So, at about the same time that Thomas Paine crossed from England to France, Lafayette tried to leave his army command and escape to Belgium. He was captured by the Austrians, who had declared war on France. Lafayette would spend several years in an Austrian prison.

Thomas Paine knew that Lafayette had played a critical role in ensuring victory for the Continental

Lafayette in the French Revolution

We know Lafayette as one of the great heroes of the American Revolution. But he also played an important role in the French Revolution.

When the French Revolution began, Lafayette was one of the moderates. He believed in reforming the nation and its government. But he also believed in protecting the king and the queen. On one occasion, he went to Versailles, leading the National Guard, to protect Louis XVI and Marie Antoinette from an angry mob.

Lafayette's popularity peaked in 1790. He led thousands of men in an emotional ceremony on the Field of Mars. They swore an oath of allegiance to the new constitution and to the nation.

One year later, Lafayette's popularity began to slip. People identified him with the king and the queen and the

Army in the final days of the American Revolution, and he wanted to do something for Lafayette. There was another imprisoned Frenchman Paine also felt that he needed to help—a Frenchman even more important than Lafayette. Paine felt strongly that he needed to do his best to protect King Louis XVI.

old system of government. Lafayette tried, but failed, to recapture the support of his fellow Frenchmen. Despairing over the situation, he went to the battlefront as a general in the war against Austria.

In 1792, Lafayette left his men. He tried to escape to neutral Belgium. But he was captured by the Austrians, and imprisoned for the next five years. He was released from prison long after Thomas Paine was set free.

Like Paine, Lafayette was injured by his time in prison. But he remained an outspoken voice for justice and liberty. Lafayette and Paine also shared one other trait: neither of them liked the French leader who assumed power when the revolution had ended—Napoleon Bonaparte.

DEFENDING THE KING

Once Austria and Prussia declared war on France, the
Parisians came to detest King Louis XVI. A mob
broke into his home and found the letters he had
exchanged with the kings of Austria and Prussia.
These treasonous letters proved King Louis would go
back against the Revolutionary cause whenever he
could. Soon, the king was in jail, and toward the end
of 1792, he was put on trial for crimes against the
people of France.

King Louis XVI had no better friend in the National
Convention than Thomas Paine. This seems strange,
since Paine had openly criticized the monarchy, and the
French king. But Thomas Paine saw, correctly, that
nothing was to be gained by putting the king to death.
Better, far better, Paine believed, to send the king into
exile, or keep him in prison until the war with Austria
and Prussia was won.

Thomas Paine made the argument during the king's
trial. Despite Paine's pleas, the king was found guilty.
After this verdict, the National Convention debated the
king's punishment. Thomas Paine argued long and hard
for exile or prison, but he lost. The king was sentenced
to death by a very narrow vote.

On January 21, 1793, King Louis XVI was executed in the center of Paris. A new age had begun.

The French revolutionaries had now become the French radicals. They had a fight on their hands.

Other European nations were horrified at the king's execution. England and Spain soon joined a coalition with Austria and Prussia. By the middle of 1793, the revolutionary government in France was fighting for its life, involved in a war with four other nations.

Thomas Paine continued his work as a member of the National Convention. He was not pleased with the death of King Louis XVI, but he saw the war against four other powers as a good thing. The common people and the soldiers of those four nations would eventually turn against their own governments, he believed. Then there would be a worldwide revolution, and the ideas he expressed in *The Rights of Man* would be welcomed everywhere.

Unfortunately, Paine's optimistic view was proved wrong, as the situation in France went from bad to worse.

TIME OF HORROR

First, the leaders of the National Convention appointed a 12-man group, named the Committee of Safety.

Paine chose to remain in France during the most brutal years of the French Revolution, fearing that if he attempted to flee to America he might be captured by British patrol boats. It would not be until the twentieth century that Paine would be recognized with this statue in Thetford, the English town where he lived as a boy.

Led by Robespierre, these 12 men became the real rulers of France.

Second, in order to keep the population happy, Robespierre and the Committee of Safety began to round up noblemen and noblewomen everywhere. These people were thrown into jail, regardless of whether or not they had done anything wrong. Their true crime was that they were of noble birth.

Third, the guillotine began to be used on an every-day basis. The guillotine was a tool used for execution. It contained a sharp blade that descended from about 20 feet in the air. The sharp blade was released by a handle or trigger on the ground, and the blade came down, neatly slicing off the person's head.

The guillotine had been intended as a humane device, since it would prevent the use of a heads-man's axe. Headsmen often did not succeed in cutting off the condemned person's head on the first try, and they had to swing again and again. The guillotine certainly removed that problem, but it also made it easy to execute a large number of people, with a minimum of effort.

The executions began in the summer of 1793. Paine saw some of the executions. He knew how terrible the

French Revolution had become. Some of his friends urged him to flee again, to leave for America. But Paine knew that the British navy controlled the Atlantic Ocean, and he feared that he would be picked up by one of the British patrol ships. Better to stay in France, he thought.

Toward the end of 1793, Thomas Paine had nearly completed his next book, *The Age of Reason*. Almost as he was about to send the manuscript to the printer, he was arrested as an enemy of France. Paine was sent to the Luxembourg Prison, where he joined hundreds of other prisoners.

Life was not bad, at first. The governor of the Luxembourg Prison was a kind man who did all he could for the comfort of the prisoners. Nonetheless, the prisoners knew that when they heard the roll of wagon wheels approaching, some of them would be taken off for a short trial and then led to the guillotine.

Thomas Paine lived in this uncertainty for nearly eight months. Many of his friends and fellow inmates were carted off to the guillotine. Even the great revolutionary leader Danton arrived at Luxembourg Prison. He had a short talk with Thomas Paine, telling him that he would fight for his life at his trial. But

Danton's efforts were not enough. He, too, perished at the guillotine.

During this terrible time, which the French called "The Terror," Robespierre's power increased. He became the virtual dictator of France. He abolished the old calendar, with its emphasis on religious festivals, and created a new one, based on what was described as the "Rule of Reason." Thomas Paine was deeply unhappy to learn that his own writings, in *The Age of Reason*, were being used by this tyrant.

Finally, as if by a miracle, Robespierre fell from power. He was accused of treason, in the National Convention, and was guillotined the next day. The great Terror was finally over.

Test Your Knowledge

I   When Paine arrived in Paris, he tried to help
the Marquis de Lafayette, who was in prison
in which country?
   a. France.
   b. Austria.
   c. Belgium.
   d. America.

2   In addition to Lafayette, Paine wanted to help
which other imprisoned Frenchman?
   a. Robespierre.
   b. Danton.
   c. Marat.
   d. King Louis XVI.

3   By mid-1793, France was involved in a war
with which nation or nations?
   a. Austria and Prussia.
   b. England.
   c. Spain.
   d. All of the above.

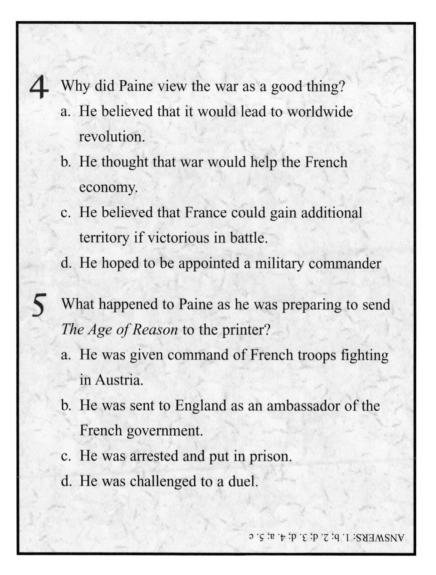

4 Why did Paine view the war as a good thing?

a. He believed that it would lead to worldwide revolution.

b. He thought that war would help the French economy.

c. He believed that France could gain additional territory if victorious in battle.

d. He hoped to be appointed a military commander

5 What happened to Paine as he was preparing to send *The Age of Reason* to the printer?

a. He was given command of French troops fighting in Austria.

b. He was sent to England as an ambassador of the French government.

c. He was arrested and put in prison.

d. He was challenged to a duel.

ANSWERS: 1. b; 2. d; 3. d; 4. a; 5. c

Home Everywhere, Home Nowhere

Thomas Paine was released from Luxembourg Prison in August 1794. He came out looking more dead than alive. This was true for most of the prisoners. They had lived under such fear, such terror, that many had lost their minds.

Thomas Paine had not lost his mind. But it could be said that he was never the same again.

First and foremost, he was bitter that more had not been done to help him. He was very angry with the American ambassador to France. Gouverneur Morris had been Paine's political foe in America, and now he had done little to help Paine while he was in prison.

Paine's anger toward Gouverneur Morris was probably justified. But Paine also turned his anger on another target: President George Washington.

Thomas Paine had not seen George Washington for about ten years. In that time, Washington had been elected the first president of the United States. Washington was the great and popular leader of the young republic, and its citizens were outraged when they learned of Paine's criticism of their president.

In an open letter to President Washington, sent in 1795, Thomas Paine attacked the president for doing nothing to rescue him from Luxembourg Prison. Paine overlooked the fact that President Washington had also done nothing to rescue his close friend and aide, Lafayette, who was then in an Austrian prison.

Paine's open letter to Washington was one of the worst mistakes he ever made. Americans loved and revered Washington. For Paine to attack him, even in a letter, meant that many Americans would never again remember Paine's great writing, and instead would associate him with unjustified criticism of the American president.

Paine's name soon became a subject of ridicule, and expressions like "Mad Tom," "Mad Tom Paine," and "the apostle of Reason and the enemy of Washington" were a common way of referring to the former hero. Nothing Paine had ever done caused him as much grief as this attack on President Washington.

Paine spent the next six years living in France. He was now truly an exile. England would never allow him to return. Americans were upset with him, to say the least. France allowed him to stay, but his remarks were no longer reported in the press, and many people made fun of him.

FREE PASSAGE HOME

It took time, and a change in presidential leadership, for Paine to begin the slow process of restoring his good name. It all began when Thomas Jefferson was elected the third president of the United States.

Thomas Jefferson won a tough campaign. He defeated the incumbent president, John Adams, and Aaron Burr in a close election. By the time Jefferson assumed the presidency in 1801, Washington was dead. Jefferson could now do something for Thomas Paine.

Jefferson and Paine had always been friendly. They believed in many of the same things, and had written letters to each other about religious, scientific, and political matters. In 1802, Thomas Jefferson offered Thomas Paine free passage home on an American ship.

The word "free" was important because Paine was greatly in debt. Even though he had written three great bestsellers in his lifetime (*Common Sense, The Rights of Man,* and *The Age of Reason*), he had never been good at managing money or keeping it. He was desperate for funds. He accepted President Jefferson's offer.

Thomas Paine sailed across the Atlantic one more time. He arrived in Philadelphia, where he was greeted more with scowls than with cheers. Despite Jefferson's intervention, Americans still remembered what Paine had written about George Washington. Many of them were also angry that he had abandoned the cause of liberty in America to fight for it in England and France.

Paine went to Washington, D.C. It was then a very small place, with a regular population of less than one thousand persons, and had only recently become the new capital of the United States. But President Thomas Jefferson was there, and Paine felt certain of a welcome from him, and perhaps a post in the government.

Paine tried, but failed, to interest the government in his new projects. He still talked and wrote about iron

The Federalists and the Republicans

The Federalists and the Republicans were the first two political parties in the United States. The Federalists believed in a strong national government. The Republicans believed in the rights of the individual states to make most of the laws that concerned them.

The two political parties first emerged during the presidency of George Washington. Different opinions about the way America should be governed split the members of Washington's own cabinet. Secretary of the Treasury Alexander Hamilton and Vice-President John Adams favored an active federal government, an economy that supported industrial development, and a foreign policy that was pro-Britain. This position became known

bridges. President Jefferson was polite, but he was busy with many things, and could not pay much attention to scientific matters. Giving up, Paine finally left Washington. He went to Philadelphia, and then to New York City.

It was in New York that Paine finally found a warm welcome. There were many recent British immigrants in New York. They had read *The Age of Reason* and *The Rights of Man*. To them, Paine was a great hero

as federalist, and those who supported it were labeled Federalists. Secretary of State Thomas Jefferson favored a more limited role for the federal government, suggesting that the government should not play an active part in the nation's economy. He favored a foreign policy that was pro-France. His supporters became known as Anti-Federalists or Republicans.

In the election of 1796, the strong differences between the parties became clear. The 1796 election is considered by many to be the first "real" election—an election in which candidates with different views of how the country should be run actively campaigned. In the end, Federalist John Adams was elected president.

and, for a time, he enjoyed being the guest at parties and receiving invitations to speak.

FINAL YEARS

Finally, Paine left New York City and traveled the short distance to New Rochelle. A plot of land and a farmhouse had been given to him in the 1780s. After many years of travel and exile, he was at last able to settle into a routine life on that piece of land.

The times were not good for Paine. Even though Jefferson was president, the nation had become more conservative since the American Revolution. Some people remembered Paine fondly, for what he had done in the past, but others viewed him only as the man who had fled America at an important time and then had dared to criticize the president from a safe distance.

Paine did not help matters. Both in his appearance and his attitude, he had become harder and more difficult. He became sloppy, seldom bothering to wash himself or his clothes. And when he met people who disagreed with him, Paine could be as aggressive and demanding as ever.

The very lowest point came in 1807. Thomas Paine went into the town of New Rochelle to vote.

Paine spent his final years in New York. He lived for
several years in New Rochelle, where the Thomas Paine
Monument now stands.

The registrars behind the booth refused to let him vote, since he was, they said, not an American citizen. Paine tried to fight his way through this block but failed.

In despair, Paine left his farm and New Rochelle. He moved to New York City and lived in a rooming house. It was there that Thomas Paine died on June 8, 1809.

Six people attended his funeral. Paine had known Franklin, Washington, Adams, and most of the other great leaders of the American Revolution. He had spent time with Lafayette, Danton, Marat, Robespierre, and the leaders of the French Revolution. Yet only a handful of people mourned his death.

Was there no justice? Not for Thomas Paine.

He was seldom remembered, even in tributes to the heroes of the American Revolution. The final indignity came about ten years after his death. A British journalist came to America, broke into the New Rochelle cemetery, and dug up and stole Thomas Paine's bones. This journalist intended to make an exhibit of them in England, but the bones were lost after his death.

Truly, Thomas Paine belonged everywhere and nowhere at the same time. He was one of the great men of his time, but he was unable to make that greatness work for him.

Paine has found some honor in modern times. His name is well regarded today, in the twenty-first century. His faults are largely forgotten, and he is instead seen as one of the prophets of liberty, someone who fought for that cause in England, France, and America.

Test Your Knowledge

I Who did Paine publicly criticize for not helping him while he was in prison?

a. The British king.

b. Robespierre.

c. George Washington.

d. Thomas Jefferson.

2 Which president offered Paine free passage to America?

a. John Adams.

b. Thomas Jefferson.

c. George Washington.

d. James Madison.

3 Which American city offered Paine a warm welcome?

a. New York.

b. Philadelphia.

c. Washington, D.C.

d. Boston.

4 In 1807, Paine tried to vote but was refused. Where did this happen?

a. Philadelphia.

b. Washington, D.C.

c. New Rochelle, New York.

d. Buffalo, New York.

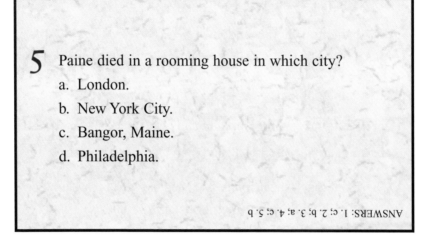

5 Paine died in a rooming house in which city?

  a. London.

  b. New York City.

  c. Bangor, Maine.

  d. Philadelphia.

ANSWERS: 1. c; 2. b; 3. a; 4. c; 5. b

1737   Thomas Paine is born in Thetford, England.

1757   Paine travels to London.

1762   Paine enters the British excise service.

1772   Paine publishes a pamphlet on the excise officers.

1774   Paine leaves England and sails to America.

1775   Paine works for *Pennsylvania Magazine.*

1776   Paine publishes *Common Sense*; serves as a volunteer in the American army; publishes *The Crisis.*

1777   Paine serves the Continental Congress as a secretary.

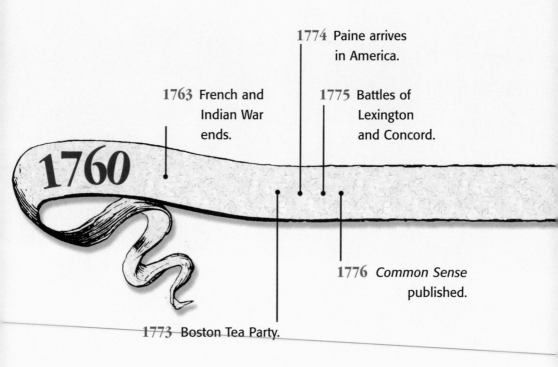

1774 Paine arrives in America.

1763 French and Indian War ends.

1775 Battles of Lexington and Concord.

1760

1776 *Common Sense* published.

1773 Boston Tea Party.

1778   Paine is involved in the Silas Deane Affair; is removed from his job at the Continental Congress.

1780   Paine publishes *Public Good.*

1781   Paine is in France for five months before returning to America.

1782   George Washington hires Paine to write for the new government.

1787   Paine sails for France.

1788   Paine leaves France for England.

1789   The French Revolution begins.

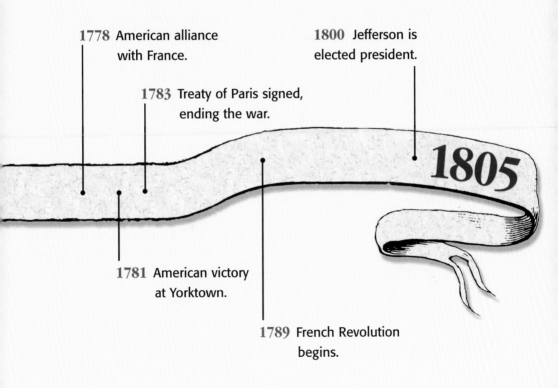

1778 American alliance with France.

1800 Jefferson is elected president.

1783 Treaty of Paris signed, ending the war.

1805

1781 American victory at Yorktown.

1789 French Revolution begins.

1790 Burke publishes *Some Thoughts Concerning the Revolution in France.*

1791 Paine publishes *The Rights of Man.*

1792 Paine becomes a delegate to the National Convention in France.

1793 Paine argues against the execution of King Louis XVI; is thrown in jail in Paris.

1794 *The Age of Reason* is published.

1795 Paine attacks President Washington in an open letter.

1799 Napoleon Bonaparte becomes the new leader of France.

1800 Thomas Jefferson wins the American presidential election.

1802 Paine returns to the United States on a government ship.

1803 Paine retires to New Rochelle, New York.

1807 Paine is barred from voting in an election.

1809 Paine dies in New York City on June 8.

Notes

CHAPTER 1
The Crisis

1 Thomas Paine, *Thomas Paine: Collected Writings* (New York: The Library of America, 1995), 91.
2 Ibid.
3 Ibid.
4 Ibid.

CHAPTER 2
English Youth

5 Quoted in Bartlett, *Famous Quotations* (Boston: Little, Brown and Company, 1980).
6 Quoted in David Freeman Hawke, *Paine* (New York: Harper & Row, 1974), 20.

CHAPTER 3
The Newest American

7 Ibid.
8 Ibid., 28.
9 Ibid., 33.
10 Paine, 6–7.
11 Ibid., 12.
12 Ibid., 53–54.
13 Quoted in Thomas J. Fleming, ed., *Affectionately Yours, George Washington* (New York: W.W. Norton, 1967), 101.

CHAPTER 8
The Rights of Man

14 Paine, 443–444.

Bibliography

Fast, Howard. *Citizen Tom Paine*. New York: Duell, Sloan & Pearce, 1943.

Fleming, Thomas. J., ed. *Affectionately Yours, George Washington*. New York: W.W. Norton, 1967.

Hawke, David Freeman. *Paine*. New York: Harper & Row, 1974.

Paine, Thomas. *Thomas Paine, Collected Writings*. New York: The Library of America, 1995.

Williamson, Audrey. *Thomas Paine: His Life, Work and Times*. London: George Allen & Unwin, 1973.

Ayer, A.J. *Thomas Paine*. New York: Atheneum, 1988.

Liell, Scott. *46 Pages*. Philadelphia: Running Press, 2003.

McCartin, Brian. *Thomas Paine: Common Sense and Revolutionary Pamphleteering*. New York: Power Kids Press, 2002.

Vail, John J. *Thomas Paine*. Philadelphia: Chelsea House, 1990.

Wilson, Jerome D. *Thomas Paine*. Boston: Twayne Publishers, 1989.

WEBSITES

Complete Works of Thomas Paine
www.ushistory.org/paine

The History Guide
www.historyguide.org/intellect/paine.html

Text of *Common Sense*
www.constitution.org/tp/comsense.htm

Thomas Paine National Historical Association
www.thomaspaine.org

Index

Index

Index

Index

About the Author

SAMUEL WILLARD CROMPTON lives in the Berkshire Hills of western Massachusetts. He is the author or editor of more than 30 books, many of them for young adults. He has contributed to several Chelsea House series, and is also the author of *John Adams* in the LEADERS OF THE AMERICAN REVOLUTION series. Mr. Crompton is a major contributor to the *American National Biography*, published by Oxford University Press. He teaches American history and Western civilization at Holyoke Community College in Massachusetts.